# 2018-2019

# Be Strong

## Circuit Assembly
### of
## Jehovah's Witnesses

designed by:
@JWDownloads

**CIRCUIT ASSEMBLY PROGRAM WITH BRANCH REPRESENTATIVE**

Personal goals 2018 - 2019

Spiritual goals 2018 - 2019

My favorite speaker:

Most memorable point:

My favorite talk:

New points to use in ministry:

Location:

Attendance:

Comment/Note:

# 10:00 Jehovah - Our Source of "Strength and Power"

**Speaker/Congregation**

**Favorite Point**

How does Joshua 1:9 encourage you?

**Scriptures/Main Points**

- _____
- _____
- _____
- _____
- _____
- _____

**Notes**

How has Jehovah shown that He is MY source of strength and power?

Jehovah - Our Source of "Strength and Power"

# 10:15 Be Strong - Build Your Faith

**Be Strong - Build Your Faith**

*Speaker/Congregation:*

*Talk Summary:*

*Favorite Point:*

*TO USE IN MINISTRY:*

| SCRIPTURE + NOTE | SCRIPTURE + NOTE |
|---|---|
| SCRIPTURE + NOTE | SCRIPTURE + NOTE |

## Notes

# 10:30 Be Strong - Zealously Preach, Teach, and Train

Speaker + Congregation

Speaker's teaching skills I want to imitate

Apply in MY LIFE

Ways I am already zealous:

How I can improve:

Notes

Be Strong - Zealously Preach, Teach, and Train

# 11:05 From a Weak State, Be Made Powerful!

Speaker + Congregation:

**From a Weak State, Be Made Powerful!**

| Scripture + Note | Scripture + Note | Scripture + Note | Scripture + Note |
|---|---|---|---|
| | | | |

**How I can become powerful:**

**How I can help others to Be Made Powerful:**

| Main Points • Scriptures | Notes |
|---|---|
| ∞ | |
| ∞ | |
| ∞ | |
| ∞ | |
| ∞ | |
| ∞ | |
| ∞ | |

# 11:35 Dedication and Baptism

| Speaker/Congregation | Most encouraging point: |
| --- | --- |
| Favorite Point | Something NEW I learned: |

## Notes

How am I showing Jehovah that he is first in my life?

Dedication and Baptism

Speaker

Congregation

## 1:35 Experiences

I am grateful for:

Most moving experience for me personally:

| Names | Experience |
|---|---|
| | |
| | |
| | |

Experiences

I am motivated to:

## 2:15 SYMPOSIUM
## Be Strong - Uphold Jehovah's Sovereignty
## AS A YOUTH

**Speaker:**_____  **Congregation:**_____

**Talk Summary:**_____

_____

**Meaningful Scripture + Note:**_____

_____

**How does a person uphold Jehovah's sovereignty?**_____

_____

**Notes:**_____

_____

_____

_____

_____

_____

_____

_____

_____

_____

_____

_____

**How I will uphold Jehovah's sovereignty:**

SYMPOSIUM: Be Strong - Uphold Jehovah's Sovereignty - As A Youth

**SYMPOSIUM: Be Strong – Uphold Jehovah's Sovereignty – As Marriage Mates**

## 2:15 Symposium: Be Strong – Uphold Jehovah's Sovereignty
## AS MARRIAGE MATES

| Speaker/Congregation | Favorite Point |
|---|---|
|  |  |

| Scripture + Note | Scripture + Note |
|---|---|
|  |  |

| Scripture + Note | Scripture + Note |
|---|---|
|  |  |

# 2:55 "Stand Firm in the Faith, ... Grow Mighty"

| Speaker & Congregation | FAVORITE POINT |
|---|---|
| Scripture + Note for Ministry | Talk Summary |

| Main Points | Scriptures | Notes |
|---|---|
| • | |
| • | |
| • | |
| • | |
| • | |
| • | |
| • | |

*Stand Firm in the Faith, ... Grow Mighty*

1. Where should we turn for strength and power? (Josh 1:9; Ps 68:35)

2. How can we continue to build strong faith? (Heb 11:6)

3. Why can we be confident of success in the work that Jehovah has assigned us? (Hag 2:4-9)

4. How does Jehovah strengthen us when we face serious trials? (Ps 18:6, 30; Col 4:10, 11)

5. What will help young ones and marriage mates to uphold Jehovah's sovereignty? (Matt 22:37, 39)

6. How can we "stand firm in the faith" and "grow mighty"? (1 Cor 16:13; Rom 15:5; Heb 5:11-6:1; 12:16. 17)

# 2018-2019

# Be

# Bold

## Circuit Assembly of Jehovah's Witnesses

designed by: @JWDownloads

**CIRCUIT ASSEMBLY PROGRAM WITH CIRCUIT OVERSEER**

Personal goals 2018 - 2019

Spiritual goals 2018 - 2019

My favorite speaker:

Most memorable point:

My favorite talk:

New points to use in ministry:

Location:

Attendance:

Comment/Note:

# 9:50 Jehovah Makes Us Bold

Speaker/Congregation:

Talk Summary:

Favorite Point:

TO USE IN MINISTRY:

| SCRIPTURE + NOTE | SCRIPTURE + NOTE |
|---|---|
| | |

| SCRIPTURE + NOTE | SCRIPTURE + NOTE |
|---|---|
| | |

Notes

Jehovah Makes Us Bold

# 10:05 SYMPOSIUM: Be Bold Like... ENOCH

Speaker + Congregation:

| Scripture + Note | Scripture + Note | Scripture + Note | Scripture + Note |
|---|---|---|---|
| | | | |

**Why is Enoch a good example of boldness?**

| Main Points • Scriptures | NOTES |
|---|---|
| ∞ | |
| ∞ | |
| ∞ | |
| ∞ | |
| ∞ | |
| ∞ | |
| ∞ | |

*Be Bold Like... Enoch*

*Symposium: Be Bold Like...*

# Symposium:
# Be Bold Like... MOSES

### Speaker + Congregation

### Speaker's teaching skills I want to imitate

### Apply in MY LIFE

| Talk Summary |
| --- |
|  |

| Notes |
| --- |
|  |

Symposium: Be Bold Like... Moses

# Symposium: Be Bold Like... JEHOSHAPHAT

| Speaker/Congregation | Favorite Point |
|---|---|
| | |

| Scripture + Note | Scripture + Note |
|---|---|
| | |

| Scripture + Note | Scripture + Note |
|---|---|
| | |

Jehoshaphat

Symposium: Be Bold Like... Jehoshaphat

# SYMPOSIUM: Be Bold Like... PETER

Speaker:_____ Congregation:_____

Talk Summary:_____

_____

Scripture + Note to review for Family Worship:_____

_____

**How can we muster up boldness?:**_____

_____

Notes:_____

_____

_____

_____

_____

_____

_____

_____

_____

_____

_____

_____

How is Peter an excellent example of boldness?

# 11:15 Muster Up Boldness in the Ministry

**Muster Up Boldness in the Ministry**

| Speaker & Congregation | FAVORITE POINT |
|---|---|
| Scripture + Note for Ministry | Talk Summary |

| Main Points \| Scriptures | Notes |
|---|---|
| • | |
| • | |
| • | |
| • | |
| • | |
| • | |
| • | |

My new goals for the ministry after hearing this talk:

Speaker

Congregation

# Dedication and Baptism

BEST POINT!

Listen for a new point in this Dedication talk:

| Scriptures | Notes |
|---|---|
|  |  |
|  |  |
|  |  |
|  |  |

Dedication and Baptsim

# 1:30 Public Bible Discourse: Take Your Stand for True Worship

**Speaker/Congregation**

**Favorite Point**

**How will I "take my stand"?**

**Scriptures/Main Points**

- _____
- _____
- _____
- _____
- _____
- _____

**Notes**

This talk has motivated me to:

**Public Bible Discourse: Take Your Stand for True Worsihp**

## 2:40 Symposium: Imitate Christ's Boldness When Facing Pressure - IN THE FAMILY
### Speaker + Congregation

Speaker's teaching skills I want to imitate

Apply in MY LIFE

What pressures could I face in my family and how will I imitate Christ's boldness?

Notes

Symposium: Imitate Christ's Boldness When Facing Pressure - IN THE FAMILY

**Symposium: Imitate Christ's Boldness When Facing Pressure... IN SCHOOL**

| Speaker & Congregation | FAVORITE POINT |
|---|---|
| HOW TO BE BOLD AT SCHOOL | Talk Summary |

| Main Points \| Scriptures | Notes |
|---|---|
| • _____ | _____ |
| • _____ | _____ |
| • _____ | _____ |
| • _____ | _____ |
| • _____ | _____ |
| • _____ | _____ |
| • _____ | _____ |

*What pressures do young ones face at school, and how do they respond with boldness?*

_____

_____

**Symposium: Imitate Christ's Boldness When Facing Pressure - IN SCHOOL**

# Symposium: Imitate Christ's Boldness When Facing Pressure...
## AT WORK

Speaker + Congregation:

| Scripture + Note | Scripture + Note | Scripture + Note | Scripture + Note |
|---|---|---|---|
| | | | |

What are examples of pressures I could face at work? How will I show boldness?

| Main Points • Scriptures | Notes |
|---|---|
| ∞ | |
| ∞ | |
| ∞ | |
| ∞ | |
| ∞ | |
| ∞ | |
| ∞ | |

Symposium: Imitate Christ's Boldness When Facing Pressure - AT WORK

## SYMPOSIUM: IMITATE CHRIST'S BOLDNESS WHEN FACING PRESSURE IN THE COMMUNITY

Speaker/Congregation:

Talk Summary:

Favorite Point:

*WHAT ARE EXAMPLES OF PRESSURES I COULD FACE IN MY COMMUNITY?*

| SCRIPTURE + NOTE | SCRIPTURE + NOTE |
|---|---|
| | |
| SCRIPTURE + NOTE | SCRIPTURE + NOTE |
| | |

### Notes

*Symposium: Imitate Christ's Boldness When Facing Pressure - IN THE COMMUNITY*

**Speaker**

**Congregation**

# 3:40
# Your Boldness
# "Will Be Richly
# Rewarded"

BEST POINT

What rewards do we have to look forward to?

| Scriptures | Notes |
|---|---|

1. Why can we confidently ask Jehovah for boldness? (Ps 138:3)

2. How can we be bold like faithful servants of God in the past? (Acts 4:31)

3. How can we muster up boldness in the ministry? (1 Thess 2:2)

4. What enables us to act boldly when facing pressure? (1 Pet 2:21-23)

5. What rewards will our Christian boldness bring? (Heb 10:35)

1. Why can we confidently ask Jehovah for boldness? (Ps 138:3)

www.ingramcontent.com/pod-product-compliance
Lightning Source LLC
Chambersburg PA
CBHW051311020426
42331CB00020B/3500